HERBS

THE NEW PLANT LIBRARY

HERBS

SUSIE WHITE

Consultant: Deni Bown

Photography by Andrea Jones

LORENZ BOOKS

For Daphne and Henry, my parents

First published by Lorenz Books
an imprint of Anness Publishing Limited
Hermes House, 88–89 Blackfriars Road, London SE1 8HA

© Anness Publishing Limited 1999

Published in the USA by Lorenz Books
Anness Publishing Inc., 27 West 20th Street, New York, NY 10011
(800) 354-9657

This edition distributed in Canada by Raincoast Books
8680 Cambie Street, Vancouver, British Columbia V6P 6M9

A CIP catalogue record for this book is available from the British Library

ISBN 1 85967 901 3

Publisher Joanna Lorenz
Editor Margaret Malone
Designer Michael Morey
Photographer Andrea Jones

Printed and bound in Hong Kong/China

1 3 5 7 9 10 8 6 4 2

Publisher's note:
This book is intended as a source of information on herbs and their uses, not as a practical guide to self-medication. Neither the
author, nor the publisher can be held responsible for any specific individual's reactions, harmful effects or claims arising from the use
of the general data and suggestions it contains. Nor is any responsibility taken for mistaken identity of any of the plants. Many plants
are poisonous, all can be toxic if used inappropriately, and the advice of a qualified medical practitioner should always be sought
before using any herbal treatments or remedies. The use of any information contained in this book is entirely at the reader's own risk.

■ HALF TITLE PAGE
Lady's mantle, comfrey and mullein
■ FRONTISPIECE
Golden lemon balm
■ TITLE PAGE
Knot garden

■ LEFT
Fennel tea
■ OPPOSITE LEFT
Silver cotton lavender
■ OPPOSITE RIGHT
Coriander

Contents

Introduction

The world of herbs is a sensuous world of enormous variety, giving pleasure and enjoyment to all who enter it. Beauty of foliage and flower, countless scents and tastes, cures for various ailments: herbs offer all these things and more.

You can grow herbs in special parts of the garden, creating separate beds for individual varieties for easy picking, or combine them with cottage-garden flowers to create a wonderful relaxed atmosphere. The beauty of herbs is that they blend perfectly with all kinds of design, from the strictly formal with neatly clipped box hedging to the informality of the cottage garden. Let the sumptuous photographs and clear, practical text of this book inspire you to cultivate, harvest and enjoy these rewarding and varied plants.

■ RIGHT
A wicker basket overflows with beautiful herbs: angelica, bistort, roses and the large, silvery leaves of cardoon.

What is a herb?

■ BELOW
A variety of herbs for different uses:
lavender for scent, comfrey for healing and
marjoram and thyme in pots for cooking.

Experts differ in their interpretation of the word 'herb'. Some authorities would narrow the definition of a herb to plants used in medicine and cooking, but my favourite definition of a herb describes it as a useful plant. Herbs may supply flavourings for the cook, oils for the aromatherapist, and foliage and flowers for the gardener. We may use them for herb teas, for making pot-pourri and cosmetics, or for dyeing wool and other natural fibres. Scented plants are often grown in herb gardens, so some that are grown just for their perfume are also included here.

Some plants have just one specific use, like the teasel whose prickly head raises the nap on cloth, but that one use defines it as a herb. In fact, a herb can be a tree, shrub, herbaceous perennial or an annual, and what is harvested – a leaf, flower, stem, seed or root – may be different with each one. There has recently been a great resurgence of interest in herbs, and many have become economically important. Scientific research has led to new herb-based products, while cooking programmes on television have created a demand for more exotic herbs and edible flowers. Foreign travel, too, has whetted our appetites for a wide range of cooking styles,

and more people want to recreate the dishes they enjoyed on holiday.

From the earliest times plants have also been utilized for healing, and thousands of years later we are still benefitting from their medicinal qualities. This is just one reason why it is so vitally important that the wild places in the world are conserved. Cures for serious diseases may be waiting to be unlocked from rainforest plants which will be lost to us forever if such areas are destroyed. Fortunately, botanic gardens around the world collect wild seed, and grow and display the resulting plants, devoting areas to their native flora. By visiting them we can learn about the wild plants of our own country, as well as those from far-away places.

■ BELOW (INSET)
Rose petals have been used for centuries for making scented pot-pourri, rose water and cosmetics.

■ BELOW
The vivid petals of nasturtium make a colourful salad for *al fresco* eating.

The history of herbs

A staple ingredient in every kitchen, garlic was given to the builders of the pyramids to keep them fit.

Civilizations all over the world have used herbs since prehistory, and many traditions exist, each employing plants in different ways. The first written accounts of herbalism in the West occur in early Egyptian and Sumerian civilizations, in which the power of plants played an important role in the ceremonies of death. Anise and marjoram were employed in

mummification, while a daily dose of onion and garlic kept the builders of the pyramids healthy.

The Greeks built on the Egyptian's knowledge; Hippocrates establishing the first Western scientific system of medicine in the fifth century BC, using some 400 drugs mostly derived from herbs. Plants also played an important part in the everyday life of the Romans in terms of food flavourings, sweetly scented gardens and sacred offerings.

In the East, the first written texts date from 2,500 BC, chronicling the herbal traditions of China and

■ RIGHT
Herbs have long
been valued for
their medicinal
properties and
have provided the
blueprint for many
modern drugs.

■ OPPOSITE
FAR LEFT
Knowledge of
plants was handed
down in the form
of beautifully
illustrated books
called herbals.

Ayurveda in India. Chinese herbalism aims to restore harmony and balance, with herbs being prescribed alongside acupuncture and massage techniques. Over the centuries, the Chinese became highly skilled at incorporating many different herbs into one prescription. Ayurvedic medicine sees illness as an imbalance and seeks to restore this holistically through herbs and diet as well as massage.

After the collapse of the Roman Empire, herbalism continued in the monasteries of Europe, and information was passed down in beautifully illustrated manuscripts

called herbals. Their physic gardens grew the plants used in healing, and the knowledge spread from these to blend with the folk remedies of the countryside. New plants arrived from the East Indies and North America from the seventeenth century onwards, while the first European settlers introduced their native plants to the Americas.

These early settlers subsequently discovered Native American herbalism with its ritualistic shamanism and plant practices. In time scientific knowledge grew, and by the twentieth century many drugs

were being produced from synthesized materials, the original blueprints having been provided by the plants.

In 1931 Mrs Grieve published in England her extremely comprehensive *A Modern Herbal*, containing over 1,000 English and American plants, which helped keep interest in herbs alive at a time when they were in danger of becoming sidelined. Over the last 30 years herbs have made a great comeback and information is available through specialist herb societies, nursery growers and on the internet.

Growing herbs

In the 1950s, if people grew herbs at all, they were tucked away in some quiet corner by the vegetable garden, to be brought into the house with freshly dug potatoes. Over the last few decades interest in herbs has burgeoned and they have spread into every part of the garden. They can now be found scattered throughout flower borders, nestling among the bricks of a terrace and filling clay pots.

Their pleasures are many, ranging from the heady scent of lavender on a summer's day and the sweetness of angelica sucked straight from the stem, to borage flowers floating on a fruit-filled drink. If left to self-seed, herbs can pop up anywhere in the garden. They can provide some amazing combinations. Their casual nature makes self-seeding herbs fit delightfully into a cottage-garden layout, where marjoram, mullein, feverfew, fennel and borage can mingle with roses and bedding plants. Yet herbs are equally at home in the formal garden, the bushes clipped into topiary shapes and mounds, edging the length of a path or filling the spaces in box parterres. The knot garden of Elizabethan England, that intricate pattern of low herb hedges, is now as popular as ever.

However, when herbs are not mixed with other plants, they have enough variety of foliage and habit to create interest by themselves. It helps, though, if a herb garden is created around a theme. This might be a

■ RIGHT
Once relegated to the vegetable garden, chives are attractive enough to be planted in flower borders.

cook's garden with wooden planks edging beds packed with herbs for the kitchen. Or it could be an aromatic garden, the scented plants ready for picking and drying for pot-pourris. Themes abound: you could create a veterinary garden of plants used for treating animals, a garden of herbs used by the Romans or a colour-themed garden of gold and silver herbs. A formal design could show those plants mentioned in the Bible or by Shakespeare. A witches' garden might include mythological plants such as the rosetted mandrake. The ideas are limitless, the sheer versatility of herbs endless.

■ BELOW:
LEFT TO RIGHT
Three examples of happy self-seeding: the bold spiky leaves of teasel contrast delightfully with feathery fennel; the woolly leaves of mullein peep out from behind white-flowered comfrey at the base of this hedge; and a large plant of salad rocket (arugula) has grown from seed of the previous year.

Scent and colour

Abundant scent is one of the most endearing qualities of many herbs and trapping it within the confines of a wall, fence or hedge allows us to enjoy it to the full. Here, on a hot summer's day, when heat has released the plant's essential oils, we can revel in the smell of apples from chamomile, the pungency of sage and the whiff of curry from the curry plant. To scent the evening air, try purple and white sweet rocket (*Hesperis matronalis*), jasmine with its fragrant flowers and the charming night-scented stock, a highly fragrant plant, though it has no therapeutic use.

Herbs can even be planted underfoot so long as they do not get too much wear. Creeping thymes can be sown or planted in cracks between paving stones, their roots happy in sandy soil, their tops spreading to create pools of colour. Chamomile makes an uneven, wavy surface of bright green, its scent released at the merest touch. With careful preparation and maintenance it can even be planted as a raised seat set into a retaining wall, a herbal idea we can trace back to medieval days.

For many people the rose is the epitome of scent; the closely cupped blooms of old-fashioned varieties are sumptuous in their shape, colour and perfume. Roses give height and structure to the herb garden, and the reds, pinks and white combine wonderfully with the purple-blue of lavender. Many of the old historic roses have nostalgic names that conjure up times past: 'Souvenir de la Malmaison', 'Rambling Rector', 'Maiden's Blush' and 'Ispahan' to

name but a few. They need only light pruning compared with modern hybrid teas and often have attractive hips to add interest in the winter.

Other ways of achieving height in the herb garden are planting non-herb shrubs such as lilac and philadelphus purely for their scent, grouping giant herbs such as fennel, lovage and angelica at the back and growing climbing plants, such as

nasturtium and passion flower, up obelisks and beanpoles. The vigorous golden hop, though bare-stemmed in winter, makes a brilliant splash of colourful foliage, easily covering an old shed or fence. It produces hop flowers that can be dried on the vines

as wreaths, or stuffed into herb pillows to induce sleep.

Coloured foliage forms abound in herbs and can be placed together to make visually exciting contrasts. The dusky tones of purple sage look equally good next to bright golden marjoram or subtle silver cotton lavender. Feathery bronze fennel can be planted behind the white-edged leaves of variegated apple mint. And the rich deep purple of a basil can be grown next to golden sage in a colourful window box arrangement.

■ ABOVE LEFT
Sage adds colour and scent to the garden.

■ ABOVE RIGHT
The beautiful rose 'Souvenir de la Malmaison' was named after Empress Josephine's famous rose garden in France.

■ LEFT
The delicious scent of rosemary is trapped within the confines of this walled garden.

A part of nature

Awareness of the endangered natural
world outside our gardens has
become an important issue in the last
few years. As natural habitats
diminish, we need to be sure that the
seed and plants we buy come from
nursery sources and not from the
wild, and that we use alternatives to
peat in compost to prevent damage to
peat bogs. Rather than draw on water
sources, we can also use herbs that
thrive in dry gardens.

■ LEFT
A garden pond can
provide a small
oasis for wildlife
and include the
dark-veined leaves
of the highly
scented water mint.

■ BELOW
Herbs look stunning
in pots, be it the
brilliance of these
pot marigolds or the
grace of *aloe vera*.

Furthermore, creating a wildlife garden attracts many different species of birds and animals, and this provides extra enjoyment. Lemon balm has rather unassuming white flowers that are a magnet for honey bees, and it is traditionally planted next to bee hives to guide the bees back after foraging. The botanical name reflects this: *Melissa* is the Greek for honey bee.

Herbs can also be planted for their nectar and pollen to attract butterflies and moths. The purple-flowered anise hyssop has tall blooms that attract hover flies which, in turn, prey on the aphids that can damage other

■ ABOVE
The green leaves and bright red flowers of pineapple sage add colour indoors and out.

■ LEFT
The versatility and hardiness of herbs makes them perfect for informal planting arrangements. They can be planted in any number of different pots and containers, providing a pretty focus for spare corners of the garden, window sills and roof gardens.

plants. Leaving some seedheads in the autumn attracts birds such as finches which find teasels irresistible. And water always adds an extra dimension as well as creating a habitat for frogs, toads and pondlife.

On the fringes of ponds you can plant fragrant water mint, yellow flag whose roots produce black dye, and bogbean, which is a diuretic plant.

There are many ways of bringing nature into the home; planting herbs in window boxes, in clay pots lining steps or on kitchen windowsills. Some make good and unusual houseplants: lemon verbena can be trained into a small shrub, root ginger can add a touch of the exotic, *Aloe vera* is an easily grown succulent, and pineapple sage sports its red flowers in winter.

The herb plant

Herbs come from a wide range of botanical families and visitors can learn about them in specialist gardens open to the public.

Although we often think of herbs as aromatic bushy plants that give such flavour to Mediterranean dishes, they are in fact grown all over the world. This means they originate from a wide range of habitats and come from many different botanical families.

The system by which plants are divided and classified was initiated by a Swedish botanist, Carl Linnaeus, in the eighteenth century. His genius was to group together plants that had similar characteristics so they could be identified by a botanical name which would be recognized worldwide, no matter what language you spoke. Common names can vary enormously within one country, but using Linnaeus' system of nomenclature we can be quite sure which herb we are referring to; this is particularly important with medicinal plants.

His system divides flowering plants first into families, secondly into genera and thirdly into species. The species may be further subdivided into naturally occurring subspecies, varieties and hybrids, which may be of natural or cultivated

■ LEFT
Chives, rosemary
and comfrey, all
from different
botanical families,
make an attractive
floral arrangement
when grouped
together.

■ BELOW LEFT
Lavender has two-
lipped flowers and
these place it in
the Labiatae/
Lamiaceae family.

origin. In addition, there are cultivars which are named clones. For example, the lovely golden form of lemon balm is known as *Melissa officinalis* 'All Gold', *Melissa* being the name of the genus, *officinalis* being the species and 'All Gold' the cultivar.

Lavender, thyme, sage and rosemary, and many other aromatic herbs, are all grouped together in the Labiatae/Lamiaceae family. This name denotes the flower shape which is two-lipped, and it is from the flowers, not the leaves or any other characteristic, that these groups are delineated.

To a beginner, botanical names may be confusing and irrelevant, but they can be fascinating as they reveal so much about the plant. They might

indicate where the plant comes from, its growth habit, who first discovered it and what it is used for. For example, the botanical name for rosemary is *Rosmarinus officinalis*. The first name comes from the Latin and means seaspray. In the wild, rosemary often grows on sea cliffs, happily weathering the salt-laden air. The second, or species, name indicates that it has been used in the herbalist's shop and the use of *officinalis* as the species name always shows a traditional herbal use. These names are vital for correctly identifying herbs which may have poisonous relatives of similar appearance.

Plant Catalogue

There are so many wonderful herbs we can grow and this book provides a tempting selection of some of the most loved. The emphasis is on culinary and aromatic herbs, and the medicinal qualities of a plant are listed only if they are generally considered safe to use. Growing conditions are mentioned when they are crucial to the plant's success. Where they grow in the wild is an indication of what position they need in the garden. Otherwise they are herbs that are not fussy about soil or situation. Heights are approximate only.

■ ABOVE AND LEFT

ANGELICA *ANGELICA ARCHANGELICA*

A stately herb for the back of a border with large globes of greenish-yellow flowers in summer. Angelica dies after flowering but it self-seeds plentifully, especially enjoying a semi-shaded site in moist soil. Young leaf stalks can be candied for cake decoration or cooked with tart fruits and rhubarb as a sweetener. Height 2m (6ft). Perennial.

■ OPPOSITE LEFT

BAY *LAURUS NOBILIS*

This glossy-leaved shrub has an ancient history. Bay was used by the Romans to crown their victors, and it was a strewing herb on medieval floors, its leaves having a strong aroma and antiseptic properties. Dried or fresh bay leaves have many culinary uses, ranging from flavouring soups and meats to enhancing puddings and custards. It needs a warm, sunny position and can be clipped into topiary shapes. In a large pot it grows about 1.2m (4ft) high. Tree or shrub.

■ LEFT

BASIL *OCIMUM BASILICUM*

An annual herb native to India, basil is now grown worldwide for its wonderful flavour. A vital ingredient of Mediterranean cooking, basil blends well with tomatoes, being added fresh or dried to pizza and pasta, and fresh to summer salads. Basil needs plenty of sun and protection from frost. Its tops should be pinched out to encourage bushy growth. Its green leaves are shiny and slightly puckered and it has small, creamy flowers that appear in late summer. Other varieties to try include the attractive purple basil, *O. basilicum* 'Dark Opal'; lemon basil, *O. basilicum* var. *citriodorum*; a basil with large, crinkled leaves, *O. basilicum* 'Green Ruffles'; and the sacred herb of Indian temples *O. tenuiflorum* (syn. *O. sanctum*). Height 50–70cm (20–28in). Annual.

■ ABOVE

BERGAMOT *MONARDA DIDYMA*

The sweetly aromatic leaves of bergamot resemble the scent of bergamot orange and make a refreshing herb tea. Growing wild in the North American woods, this lovely plant needs a rich, moist soil to flourish. Butterflies are attracted to its red, tubular flowers, and both flowers and leaves are dried for pot-pourri. Take internally for minor digestive problems. Height 60cm (2ft). Perennial.

■ LEFT
BOX *BUXUS SEMPERVIRENS* 'SUFFRUTICOSA'

The dense, hard wood of box has been used for centuries for wood engraving and making boxes, hence the name. In the herb garden, the dwarf cultivar *B. sempervirens* 'Suffruticosa', with its glossy, evergreen leaves, is the classic plant for edging, topiary or creating knot gardens. All parts of box are toxic if eaten. Height 75cm (2½ft). Shrub.

■ ABOVE
BORAGE *BORAGO OFFICINALIS*

Borage, with its sky-blue flowers, epitomizes sunny, summer days in the herb garden. These pretty flowers can be floated on fruit drinks or sprinkled on salads for colour. Although roughly hairy, the young leaves give a delicious cucumber flavour to drinks, and it is easy to understand its medieval reputation for making people happy. There is a beautiful but less common white-flowered form. Height 90cm (3ft). Annual.

■ RIGHT AND INSET
CARAWAY *CARUM CARVI*

Versatile caraway has feathery leaves, a tap root, and white flowers in its second summer. The leaves flavour soups and stews, the root can be cooked as a vegetable, and the strongly-flavoured seeds are used in cakes and bread or to spice cabbage, cheese, sausages and sauerkraut. Chewing the digestive seeds helps ease heartburn and if infused, the seeds help reduce colic. Height 60cm (2ft). Biennial.

■ RIGHT AND FAR RIGHT
CATMINT *NEPETA* x
FAASSENII

Aromatic catmint is grown as
a pretty edging plant where
it can sprawl and flop over
paths. It has a mass of blue
flowers in summer, softly
coloured grey leaves and
thrives in a sunny spot.
Height 60cm (2ft).
Perennial. The related, but
less showy, catnip, *Nepeta
cataria*, is the plant that cats
love to roll in, and can be
used to treat colds by
lowering fever. Height 90cm
(3ft). Perennial.

■ ABOVE
CHAMOMILE *CHAMAEMELUM NOBILE*

Chamomile has a wonderful, sweet scent, rather like apples, which is released upon
brushing its feathery, bright green leaves. Creamy white, daisy-like flowers are borne on the
end of long stems in summer, and they are made into the soothing and digestive herb tea, as
administered to Peter Rabbit! Height 15cm (6in). Perennial. A non-flowering cultivar, *C.
nobile* 'Treneague', is used to make chamomile lawns. Height 5cm (2in). Perennial.

■ ABOVE
CHERVIL *ANTHRISCUS
CEREFOLIUM*

With lacy, green leaves and a delicate,
aniseed scent, chervil is a pretty, annual
herb. Harvest before its white flowers open
in midsummer, it should always be used
fresh and added to cooking only at the last
minute to preserve its flavour. Its leaves
make a decorative garnish and freshly
chopped leaves give a lovely aniseed flavour
to salads. Height 30cm (1ft). Annual.

■ LEFT AND INSET
CHIVES *ALLIUM SCHOENOPRASUM*

Chives are an important herb, giving an onion flavour to omelettes, fish sauces, salads, cheeses and vegetables. The mauve/purple or white flowers bloom from spring onwards, their stems being pinched out to make harvesting the leaves easier. A named cultivar, 'Forescate', inset, is hardy and has deep pink flowers. The florets can be sprinkled on salads for colour and flavour. Height 15cm (6in). Perennial.

■ RIGHT AND INSET
COMFREY *SYMPHYTUM ORIENTALE*

A wild plant of damp streamsides, ditches and other wet places, comfrey has wide, rough leaves and bears white, pink or blue, bell-shaped flowers in forked, curled clusters in spring. Russian comfrey, *Symphytum* x *uplandicum*, was used as a fodder crop and there is a dramatic, cream-variegated form, 'Variegatum', that is excellent for adding colour to the border. *Symphytum officinale*, inset, is reputed to heal fractures, earning it the name of knit-bone, and it is still used as a compress for sprains and bruises. Comfrey is valued for compost making. Do not take internally. Height 50cm (20in). Perennial.

■ RIGHT

COTTON LAVENDER
SANTOLINA CHAMAECYPARISSUS

Of year-round interest, cotton lavender is a silvery, evergreen shrub for sunny, well-drained soil that can be clipped into a neat shape or dwarf hedge. Its soft, woolly leaves have a strong aroma and can be dried for pot-pourris. Yellow button flowers grow on upright stems and are easily dried for winter arrangements. Height 50cm (20in). Shrub.

■ LEFT

CORIANDER (CILANTRO)
CORIANDRUM SATIVUM

A popular culinary herb, coriander (cilantro) is an essential flavouring for Indian and other cuisines. Grown in semi-shade, it produces plenty of strong-tasting, lacy leaves popular in many dishes around the world. It has small, white flowers and when grown in full sun produces intensely flavoured seeds used in spice mixtures, sausages, breads and desserts. Height 75cm (2^1/2ft). Annual.

■ LEFT

COWSLIP *PRIMULA VERIS* AND PRIMROSE *PRIMULA VULGARIS*

Cowslips and primroses are the epitome of spring. The roots and flowers of both have similar medicinal properties, being sedative and soothing for bronchitis and other respiratory problems. The flowers can be candied or used in salads, and cowslip wine is an old country favourite. *P. veris,* shown left, – height 20cm (8in). Perennial. *P. vulgaris* – height 15cm (6in). Perennial.

■ LEFT
ELECAMPANE
*INULA
HELENIUM*

Elecampane has been used for centuries to soothe coughs and sore throats. Named after Helen of Troy, its height and shaggy, yellow daisies in summer make it an excellent back-of-the-border plant. The roots smell of violets when dug up, and are used to make throat lozenges. They can also be used as a fixative in pot-pourri. Height 2m (6ft). Perennial.

■ ABOVE
DILL *ANETHUM GRAVEOLENS*

Sown as an annual, dill looks similar to fennel but is shorter, and its feathery leaves are blue-grey rather than green. Its taste and scent are unique, with a depth and pungency that goes well with fish, especially salmon and pickled herring. Good-quality seed will be produced only in regions with long, hot summers. Successive sowings at three-to-four-week intervals during the growing season will provide plenty of leaves for cooking. The flowers are small open yellow umbels, borne in summer. The seed is an important constituent of gripe water, which is used to ease children's colic and help them to sleep. Height 90cm (3ft). Annual.

■ LEFT
EVENING PRIMROSE
OENOTHERA BIENNIS

As its name suggests, evening primrose blooms on a summer's evening, attracting night-flying moths with its large, scented, luminous flowers. Recent research has found the seeds of this herb to be high in gamma linoleic acid, and it is now widely available for conditions such as premenstrual tension, rheumatoid arthritis, multiple sclerosis and eczema. Height 90cm (3ft). Biennial.

■ RIGHT
FEVERFEW
TANACETUM PARTHENIUM

Feverfew has an intense, bitter smell and taste, cheerful, white, daisy-like flowers all summer, and self-seeds abundantly. A typical cottage-garden plant, feverfew also has attractive, golden-leaved and double-flowered forms. Its historic reputation for curing headaches has recently been borne out by medical research, and it is used for treating migraines as well as rheumatism and arthritis. It should not, however, be taken during pregnancy, and some people develop mouth ulcers from eating the fresh leaf. Height 60cm (2ft). Perennial.

■ LEFT
FENNEL
FOENICULUM VULGARE

The feathery, aniseed-flavoured leaves of fennel are excellent with fish, whether cooked in stuffed mackerel or used fresh as a pretty garnish. Cut up with kitchen scissors, fennel is delicious in sauces or added to salads. Flat, yellow umbels flower in late summer and are followed by strongly flavoured seeds. They are good for the digestion and for loss of appetite in the form of a soothing herb tea. The attractive, bronze foliage of *Foeniculum vulgare* 'Purpureum' makes it a popular border plant. Two or three clumps cut down in rotation will provide plenty of foliage for cooking. Height 2m (6ft). Perennial.

■ ABOVE
FRENCH TARRAGON
ARTEMISIA DRACUNCULUS

A classic culinary herb, French tarragon has an aniseed flavour that goes well with many dishes. A tender perennial, it needs to be propagated by cuttings as it does not set seed. Any seed offered for sale will be of the inferior, though hardier, Russian tarragon, *Artemisia dracunculus* subsp. *dracunculoïdes.* Historically used for toothache, and by the Romans to treat snakebite, French tarragon has narrow, grey-green leaves that bruise easily. It is delicious in chicken and egg dishes, in salad dressings and sauces or infused in vinegar. Height 60cm (2ft). Perennial.

HORSERADISH
ARMORACIA RUSTICANA

A fast spreader with coarse leaves, white flowers and an invasive habit, horseradish is not a beauty. Its importance, however, is hidden underground, where its white roots develop a pungency, making it delicious with meats, salad dressings and sauces. Pencil-thick roots are grated and mixed with vinegar and honey for a classic sauce. Height 90cm (3ft). Perennial.

GOOD KING HENRY
CHENOPODIUM BONUS-HENRICUS

A medieval pot herb, good King Henry has triangular, arrow-shaped leaves that can be cooked as an alternative to spinach. It makes a healthy vegetable, having a high iron content, and is best harvested in spring when tender. The flowers are yellowish-green and the plant thrives in rich, well-drained soil where it will self-seed. Height 50cm (20in). Perennial.

HYSSOP
HYSSOPUS OFFICINALIS

Hyssop is a small, aromatic, evergreen shrub that makes an attractive edging plant for the herb garden. The leaves give a warm flavour to soups and stews, oily fish and meats, aiding the digestion of fats. In summer, hyssop is covered in delightful, blue flowers that are a magnet for butterflies, as well as being edible. There are also pretty pink and white forms. Height 60cm (2ft). Shrub.

LAVENDER
LAVANDULA SPECIES

Lavender is a shrub that has been loved for centuries for its evocative scent. Branches of lavender were strewn on medieval floors to counteract unpleasant odours and deter insects, while dried lavender was used in bunches or sachets to keep moths from linen, and lavender honey was highly prized for its taste. Today, we have an exciting range of cultivars to choose from, with flower colour ranging from deep purple, through blues to pinks and whites. Lavender flowers in mid-summer and is harvested when the flowers are just opening.

■ LEFT
LAVANDULA ANGUSTIFOLIA 'HIDCOTE'

A very popular cultivar, named after the famous garden in Gloucestershire, England, this dwarf lavender has deep violet flowers in compact spikes. Height 60cm (2ft). Shrub.

■ LEFT
LAVANDULA STOECHAS

Known as French lavender, this species has curious, dark purple flowers with lighter purple bracts that crown the flower head and a slightly stronger scent than most. All lavenders are sun lovers, but this needs more protection than most to survive. Height 60cm (2ft). Shrub.

■ RIGHT
LAVANDULA VIRIDIS

An unusual, tender lavender with green leaves and tiny, white flowers with green bracts. The plant is highly aromatic with an antiseptic scent, and is sticky when handled on a hot day. Height 60cm (2ft). Shrub.

■ ABOVE LEFT AND ABOVE RIGHT
LEMON BALM *MELISSA OFFICINALIS*

Just squeezing the green leaves of lemon balm releases a lovely,
sweet, lemon scent. This easily grown herb can be cooked with fish
or used to flavour fruit salads, desserts, ice creams and jellies. It
makes a refreshing herb tea that eases nausea and colic. The
insignificant, white flowers are a powerful draw for bees, and
lemon balm was traditionally planted next to bee hives. With its
delicious, lemony scent, balm was laid on the floor of medieval
houses as a strewing herb. Two colourful cultivars make excellent
foliage plants: golden lemon balm, *M. officinalis* 'All Gold'
(pictured above right); and variegated lemon balm, *M. officinalis*
'Aurea'. Height 80cm (32in). Perennial.

■ RIGHT
LOVAGE *LEVISTICUM OFFICINALE*

One of the tallest herbs, lovage makes a sizeable clump, its shiny,
divided leaves smelling strongly of celery mixed with yeast. These
leaves give a robust flavour to soups, stews and stocks and are
especially useful in vegetarian cooking. Flat umbels of green flowers
appear on the end of tall stalks in summer. The seeds have a strong
celery taste and are used in cream cheeses, biscuits (crackers) and
breads. Height 2m (6ft). Perennial.

MARJORAM
ORIGANUM SPECIES

Marjorams are important culinary herbs but some confusion exists regarding their common names. The plant grown in England as marjoram has the botanical name *Origanum vulgare.* An extremely variable species, its growing conditions can greatly influence its flavour. When harvested in the Mediterranean, it is sold dried under the name of oregano. To add to the confusion, other herbs may also be sold as oregano, especially in the USA. The dried herb sold as marjoram is from sweet marjoram, *Origanum majorana,* and has a quite different flavour. Marjorams range in colour from purple through to white, and grow best in well-drained soil in full sun.

■ ABOVE RIGHT AND BELOW
ORIGANUM VULGARE

A variable species of marjoram, it occurs in the wild from the Azores to Taiwan and was introduced to the USA. With green leaves on strong stems and pink flowers, it is much used in Mediterranean cooking. The flowers can be eaten in salads and the flowering tops are easily dried for winter arrangements. Height 60cm (2ft). Perennial.

■ BELOW
ORIGANUM VULGARE 'AUREUM CRISPUM'

For a bright splash of gold, 'Aureum' and 'Aureum Crispum', are excellent at lighting up dull areas of the garden. The two forms are similar, though the leaves of 'Aureum Crispum' are smaller and puckered. Best grown out of full sun to avoid scorching the leaves, they can also be used in cooking. Height 45cm (1¹/2ft). Perennial.

■ BELOW
ORIGANUM VULGARE 'POLYPHANT'

A very pretty marjoram with white variegation and white flowers, named after a village in Cornwall, England, that is famous for its quarry, the stone being used in carving and church decoration. Height 45cm (1¹/2ft). Perennial.

MINT
MENTHA SPECIES

The mints have a wide range of scents and foliage colours, making them adaptable for borders, herb gardens and wilder areas of the garden. All are spreaders, some being more invasive than others, and need planting with thought, or keeping under control in a large, sunken pot. Their leaves can be harvested for adding to pot-pourris, or sprigs can be used to scent bathwater, as done by the Ancient Romans.

■ BELOW
PENNYROYAL
MENTHA PULEGIUM

Once used on medieval floors to repel fleas, pennyroyal has a reputation for keeping ants out of food cupboards. Strongly scented, with upright or floppy stems and pale purple flowers, it can be grown at the front of a herb border. Height 30cm (1ft). Perennial.

■ ABOVE LEFT
HORSEMINT
MENTHA LONGIFOLIA

A very decorative mint with soft, grey-green leaves and long, mauve flower spikes in summer, loved by bees and butterflies. It makes a good cut flower. Less a cooking herb and more a garden plant, this mint is lovely but invasive. Height 1.2m (4ft). Perennial.

■ ABOVE RIGHT
APPLEMINT
MENTHA SUAVEOLENS

A very vigorous mint, it can easily run riot in the herb garden. Applemint has soft, woolly, rounded leaves and pretty, pink flower spikes in summer. It gives a delicious flavour to boiled potatoes, and runner and broad (fava) beans. Height 90cm (3ft). Perennial.

■ RIGHT
SPEARMINT
MENTHA SPICATA

The classic herb for cooking with potatoes or making mint sauce, this is the most common of the mints. Its bright green, smooth leaves make a refreshing herb tea that aids digestion. Height 60cm (2ft). Perennial.

■ RIGHT
NASTURTIUM
TROPAEOLUM MAJUS

Widely grown as a garden annual, nasturtium leaves and flowers have a strong, biting flavour. Long, trailing or climbing stems scramble over fences or up shrubs, bearing brilliant orange, red or yellow flowers that give intense colour and a peppery flavour to summer salads. The leaves are edible and the unripe seeds can be pickled as a substitute for capers. Height up to 2m (6ft). Annual.

■ BELOW RIGHT
PARSLEY
PETROSELINUM CRISPUM

A favourite and much-grown herb, parsley is added to a wide range of culinary dishes. Soups, casseroles, fish sauces, *bouquets garnis*, garnishes and omelettes, all benefit from parsley's delicious flavour and quantities of iron and vitamin C. The flat-leaved form known as Italian or French parsley has a slightly stronger flavour. Height 60cm (2ft). Biennial.

■ FAR RIGHT
ROCKET (ARUGULA) *ERUCA*
VESICARIA SUBSP. *SATIVA*

Rocket (arugula) is an easily grown annual with an irregularly toothed leaf that is strong-smelling and has a nutty taste. Delightful in salads, it is gaining in popularity and can now be bought in supermarkets. The flowers are pretty, with yellow or cream-coloured petals and dark violet veins. It can be planted in succession throughout the season for a long crop. Height 60cm (2ft). Annual.

■ ABOVE
ROSE *ROSA* SPECIES

Since ancient times, roses have been loved and grown in gardens for their scent and colour, their petals harvested for creating long-lasting pot-pourris. They were also used in the stillroom of the medieval home where rose waters, cosmetics, oils and powders were made. Rose petals can be crystallized for cake decoration while rose water flavours ice-cream, puddings, sweets and jellies. Old-fashioned roses have the best scent, one of the most intoxicating being *R. gallica* var. *officinalis*, the apothecary's rose. Height 90cm (3ft). Shrub.

■ RIGHT
ROSEMARY *ROSMARINUS OFFICINALIS*

Rosemary likes a well-drained soil and sunny situation, reminiscent of its home in the hot scrubland of stony, Mediterranean hillsides. Just brushing against its spiky foliage will release its warm aroma. Pretty, pale blue flowers bloom in spring and can be sprinkled on salads. Sprigs of rosemary are the ideal accompaniment to roast lamb and other meat dishes, and can be steeped in olive oil for a wonderful salad dressing. Height up to 2m (6ft). Shrub.

SAGE
SALVIA SPECIES

The sages are very decorative garden plants, highly aromatic and often with beautiful foliage or flowers. To grow them successfully you must emulate their Mediterranean habitat and provide well-drained, stony soil in full sun. To prevent them from becoming leggy, prune them from the second year on, cutting back their flowering branches to just above the previous year's growth. Even so, sage is a fairly short-lived shrub, and is best replaced every four to five years.

■ ABOVE LEFT
COMMON SAGE
SALVIA OFFICINALIS

An evergreen shrub with roughly textured, grey-green leaves, this is the sage of sage and onion stuffing. In summer it bears pretty, purple flowers that attract bumble bees. Much valued as a culinary herb, it flavours the green-veined English Sage Derby cheese, meats, poultry, oily fish and sausages. It is also an essential oil used in perfumes. Height 80cm (32in). Shrub.

■ ABOVE RIGHT
GOLDEN SAGE
SALVIA OFFICINALIS 'ICTERINA'

This delightful, golden-variegated form of common sage provides an evergreen splash of colour in the herb garden, and can also be used in cooking. It is a compact plant, especially if kept pruned, and the prunings can be used as cuttings to create more plants. Height 60cm (2ft). Shrub.

■ LEFT
PURPLE SAGE
SALVIA OFFICINALIS PURPURASCENS GROUP

Another excellent foliage plant, this sage has deeply coloured dusky purple leaves and blue flowers. Some herbalists think it is useful for medicinal purposes, and it makes a very good gargle for sore throats. Height 80cm (32in). Shrub.

■ LEFT AND INSET
SORREL *RUMEX ACETOSA*

Sorrel (inset) is a rather ordinary-looking herb, but it makes a delicious soup when cooked with potatoes and onion. The leaves should be picked in spring when tender and the red flower spikes cut off in early summer to prevent self-seeding. Height 90cm (3ft). Perennial. A less acidic, more lemony flavour comes from French sorrel, *Rumex scutatus* (main picture), a lower-growing herb with spear-shaped leaves. Height 30cm (1ft). Perennial.

■ BELOW LEFT
SOAPWORT *SAPONARIA OFFICINALIS*

A typical cottage-garden plant, soapwort has scented, pale pink flowers in late summer and a running habit, making it very invasive. Long used, as its name suggests, as a cleanser, its delicate lather revitalizes old fabrics. Height 90cm (3ft). Perennial.

■ LEFT
SOUTHERNWOOD *ARTEMISIA ABROTANUM*

Shrubby southernwood has a powerful antiseptic scent with a tang of lemon, finely divided, grey-green leaves, and small, yellow flowers that emerge only in warm climates. It owes its other name of lad's love to the belief that it made beards grow! Once used to ward off plague, the leaves retain their strong scent when dried and are often put into linen sachets to repel moths. Height 90cm (3ft). Shrub.

■ RIGHT
ST JOHN'S WORT
HYPERICUM PERFORATUM

In summer, the bright yellow flowers of St John's wort emit a dark purple oil when squeezed between the fingers. The oil glands in the leaves look like small, translucent dots when held up to the light. Steeping flowers and leaves in sunflower oil for three weeks turns it red: rub on painful joints for relief. Crushing the flowers and buds between the fingers releases a wine-red pigment, hypericin, an anti-depressant, recently subjected to clinical trial.Height 60cm (2ft). Perennial.

■ FAR RIGHT
SUMMER SAVORY
SATUREJA HORTENSIS

The narrow leaves of summer savory, also known as the bean herb, have a very aromatic, warm taste that goes especially well with all kinds of beans, and pulses. Not only does it provide flavour, but it also aids digestion, easing wind; a very useful attribute in bean dishes. Height 35cm (14in). Annual.

■ RIGHT
SWEET CICELY
MYRRHIS ODORATA

A plant of streamsides and semi-shaded road verges in cooler areas, sweet cicely has a pleasing scent of aniseed which helps to distinguish it from its poisonous relatives. The finely divided green leaves often have mottled white markings at the centre. They can be cooked with rhubarb to reduce the need for sugar, and the unripe, ribbed seeds can be chopped up for salads. Height 90cm (3ft). Perennial.

■ LEFT
LEMON THYME
THYMUS x
CITRIODORUS

With a delightful lemon scent, this compact little shrub has dark green leaves and is one of the easiest to cultivate. The flowers are pale lilac, but not particularly striking. There are several cultivars with variegated foliage, marked with silver or gold for a splash of colour. Height 60cm (2ft). Shrub.

THYME
THYMUS SPECIES
There are numerous species and cultivars of thyme with scents ranging from lemon, orange and caraway to camphor and pine resin. Not all are suitable for cooking, but all make excellent, versatile garden plants. They can be grown in borders, on rock gardens, between paving slabs, on raised walls and in pots. To thrive they must have well-drained soil with gravel, and a position in full sun.

■ ABOVE
CARAWAY THYME
THYMUS HERBA-BARONA

One of the creeping thymes, this makes a slightly raised plant with dark green leaves and a strong scent of caraway. It has pale purple flowers in summer. Because of its strong flavour, it is used with the robust flavours of game or meat. Height 5cm (2in). Shrub.

■ ABOVE
BROAD-LEAVED THYME
THYMUS PULEGIOÏDES

One of the three thymes native to Britain, this low-sprawling thyme has wide, flat leaves and a pleasant scent. Because of the size of its leaves, it is easy to strip them from the stem for cooking or mixing in salads. Height 25cm (10in). Shrub.

■ ABOVE
COMMON THYME
THYMUS VULGARIS

This is the herb that most people think of as thyme when it comes to cooking. It has narrow, grey-green leaves, a strong scent, pale purple or whitish flowers in summer, and makes a good-sized shrub. Pruning after flowering helps to keep it compact. Height 60cm (2ft). Shrub.

■ ABOVE

VERVAIN

VERBENA OFFICINALIS

Vervain is a sedative herb and is sometimes used in combination with valerian – another sedative – in pill form for nervous complaints. Vervain is a much less showy herb, however, with unobtrusive, pale mauve flowers and narrow leaves. It makes a relaxing herb tea, especially for drinking after meals. Height 80cm (32in). Perennial.

■ LEFT

WELSH ONION (SCALLION)

ALLIUM FISTULOSUM

Also known as green onions, Welsh onions have hardy perennial bulbs sporting round, hollow leaves and creamy white flowers that look like rabbits' tails. They make handy vegetables, similar in flavour to onions though milder, with a long season for harvesting. The whole plant can be used. Height 30cm (1ft). Bulb.

■ BELOW

WORMWOOD

ARTEMISIA ABSINTHIUM

The silver spires of wormwood make a lovely foil to brighter colours in the flower border. Used for centuries to expel worms, especially in children, hence its name, wormwood should be treated with caution and never taken internally during pregnancy. Height 1.2m (4ft). Perennial.

■ ABOVE

WOODRUFF *GALIUM ODORATUM*

Woodruff is a lovely little woodland plant with bright green ruffs of whorled leaves on thin stems and white, starry flowers in spring. Given a rich, moist soil it can be invasive, but the rewards are cheerful spring growth and the delightful smell of new-mown hay when it is dried. It was traditionally pressed into bibles, its scent lasting for ages, and steeped in white wine for an invigorating drink. Height 50cm (20in). Perennial.

Buying herbs

The most enjoyable way to choose and buy herbs is to visit a specialist herb nursery. Many will have gardens attached where you can get inspiration from seeing how the plants are grown, as well as immediate information about their height and spread. A well-laid-out herb nursery will have clearly labelled the herbs with their common and botanical names: this is a must for correct identification. You can gain a lot of knowledge by talking to specialist growers about plants and their uses. Herb societies will be able to tell you which herb nurseries are in your area.

When visiting a nursery, look for plants that have strong-growing stems and healthy-looking foliage, and which are free from pests and diseases. Check to see if the roots are starting to grow out of the holes in the bottom of the pot. If there is a mass of roots on the outside of the pot base, the plant has probably been in the pot for too long and become pot-bound. Liverworts and weeds in the compost also tell you the plant has been in the pot too long. If there are no roots showing and the compost looks loose around the plant, it may have been very recently potted, so check with the nursery staff. Aim for a well-established plant.

Now that nurseries sell plants in containers, it is possible to buy and plant your own herbs at most times of the year. They will need very thorough watering in the summer for several weeks after planting, until they become established. In cooler areas, the Mediterranean herbs are more successful if planted in spring rather than the autumn so that they

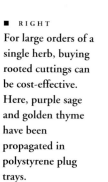

■ RIGHT
For large orders of a single herb, buying rooted cuttings can be cost-effective. Here, purple sage and golden thyme have been propagated in polystyrene plug trays.

■ BOTTOM
Herb nurseries often have attractive display gardens where you can see how big the plants will get before deciding what to buy.

have a full season to grow before encountering the winter weather. Some nurseries sell herbs by mail order, but the period during which they send out their plants is usually limited.

Buying young plants by mail order can be a cost-effective way of starting a garden. They are usually grown in plug trays (trays divided into individual modules), with a quantity of one type of herb to each tray. This is a good method when you want large amounts of one herb, when creating a chamomile or thyme lawn, for example. The big advantage of these trays is that when the plants are transferred to a pot, the roots are not disturbed, so growth is not checked.

If you are interested in growing more unusual herbs, consult the catalogues of specialist herb nurseries. On a trip to the supermarket you can add garlic bulbs to the shopping basket, breaking them into individual cloves and planting them as you would onions. Asian supermarkets can also be a good source of fresh bunches of interesting herbs, and it is possible to buy bundles of lemon grass and get them to root.

Planting outdoors

■ BELOW
Newly planted herbs laid out in a
geometric pattern around a young tree.

When deciding to create a herb
garden, the choice of plants and the
layout will be affected by the site.
The type of soil, its drainage, the
aspect, the amount of shelter and
local weather patterns will be of
paramount consideration. It always
makes sense to go with the conditions
and not against them, so a hot, dry
site will suit Mediterranean herbs,
while a heavy, moist soil needs plants
that like streams and meadows.

Looking at how a plant thrives in its
natural habitat will tell you how best
to grow it.

Begin by making a plan,
transferring measurements of the area
to be planted on to graph paper. If
you make several photocopies, you
can scribble ideas down without
worrying whether you are getting it
right the first time. Make a note of
vistas and lines of sight, especially
views from windows.

LAYING OUT AND PLANTING HERBS

1 Newly planted box trees line this
wooden-edged herb bed and provide a
framework inside which the herbs will be
laid out. First prepare the site by
thoroughly weeding and forking over to
break up the soil, then rake level.

2 Deciding how much room to give each
herb can be difficult for a beginner.
Having consulted books as to the eventual
spread of each, a helpful method is to
'draw' on the soil with sand trickled out of
a pot. If you make a mistake, it can be
easily erased and begun again.

3 Remove the herbs from their pots and
plant them carefully, with the soil
fractionally above the level at which they
were growing in the pot to allow for
settlement. If you keep the pots for reuse,
scrub them well with soap and water.

■ BELOW

Catmint thrives at the base of a warm, sunny wall in this stunning combination with the rose 'Graham Thomas' and white clematis.

4 Water each plant thoroughly and keep them watered in dry weather until they are established. Avoid planting on a hot day; just before rain is ideal.

5 In this photograph of the finished layout, you can see that the herbs have been allocated the space that they will later fill. It can be tempting to plant too close together for instant effect, but this is a mistake and will lead to overcrowding.

■ BELOW
The pink flowers of chives contrast well
with pale-coloured gravel and a dark brick
edging in this well-designed border.

Formal layouts

A formal herb design with a neat
edging of box can look stunning from
a first-floor window or balcony.
Allow plenty of room for plants that
spread, and bear in mind the eventual
heights of the herbs.

When starting, prepare the site by
eliminating all weeds, especially
perennials, digging the soil well and
raking it over. Transferring a design
to the soil can be made simple by
pouring sand out of a hole in the
bottom of a container, thus
indicating where the different blocks
of herbs go. If you make a mistake, it
is easy to start again.

Thoroughly water all pot-grown
plants several hours prior to planting,
then knock them out of their pots by
giving a sharp rap on the bottom of
the container while holding with the
other hand. Firm the soil well around
the roots after planting, water
generously, and label until you are
quite sure of the names of the
different herbs. A herb garden created
from container-grown herbs can be
planted at most times of the year,
provided it is kept well watered, but
early spring is the most sensible,
giving the plants a full season to get
established before the trials of winter.

■ BELOW
The pink flowers of chives contrast well
with pale-coloured gravel and a dark brick
edging in this well-designed border.

Planting indoors

■ BELOW
A window box can provide plenty of chives
and basil for the cook and look very
attractive as well.

Pots of herbs can look pretty set on a deep windowsill where they are handy for cooking. Choose varieties that do not grow too tall or need too much root space: mint, for example, is unsuitable unless it is divided and repotted frequently. Consider the plants' requirements for light, water and temperature: central heating can be too drying, a sunny windowsill may cause the plants to wilt, and the night temperature behind closed curtains may be too cold. Spray your herbs with water occasionally to keep the leaves fresh, and turn the pots

**SUITABLE HERBS FOR
GROWING INDOORS**

Basil

Bay (in large tubs)

Chervil

Chives

French tarragon

Marjoram

Mint

Parsley

Rosemary

Sage

Thyme

round regularly to get even light.

A conservatory offers extra possibilities because you can grow some herbs in small beds where they can spread their roots. Grown in this way, lemon verbena will make a small tree, pruned each winter to the main stem to keep it to an appropriate size. Myrtle, lavender, scented geraniums and rosemary can all be planted either in the soil or in pots. Clay pots make the best containers because they absorb moisture which helps prevent the plants from becoming waterlogged.

Planting in containers

■ BELOW

In cooler areas, tub-grown bay trees can be put out for the summer and brought indoors for protection in winter.

Even if you don't have a garden, you can still enjoy growing herbs by planting them in containers. They can be made from a great variety of materials, including terracotta, stoneware, wood and metal, or plastic imitating any of these. Any container with enough space for roots to grow and holes for drainage can be imaginatively put into service, even well-cleaned olive oil tins.

Choose the right plant for the right size container, noting the plant's eventual height and spread. If the drainage holes are not adequate, drill some more in the base of the container. Put a layer of old pottery or broken pieces of polystyrene into the bottom to stop the compost (potting soil) falling out, and fill with potting compost (potting soil). Water the plants well prior to planting and put the tallest herbs in the centre with trailing varieties around the sides. A mulch of gravel on top looks good and helps retain moisture; an

SUITABLE HERBS FOR GROWING IN CONTAINERS

Aloe vera

Basil

Bay (in large tubs)

Box

Catmint

Chamomile

Chervil

Chives

Curry plant

Lavender

Lemon verbena

Marjoram

Mint

Parsley

Rocket (arugula)

Summer and winter savory

Thyme

PLANTING A STRAWBERRY POT WITH HERBS

1 Strawberry pots have holes in the sides into which to put plants, but are also ideal for the smaller herbs: this one has eight holes plus the top. First, place some broken pottery, concave side down, in the bottom to stop the compost (potting soil) from falling through the drainage hole.

2 Fill with a layer of compost up to the level of the first holes. A soil-less compost made from peat or a peat alternative will be lighter than a soil-based one, making the pot easier to move.

important point since pots need frequent watering.

Pots can be grouped together to make attractive combinations, with the added bonus that they can be moved to create new patterns. Tender herbs can be left out to enjoy the summer sun, then brought back into the greenhouse for protection from frost. Even hanging baskets can be planted with selections of herbs, especially the coloured and variegated forms of culinary varieties.

■ LEFT
This strawberry pot has been planted entirely with different varieties of thyme, some smelling of lemon. Note the terracotta dish for ease of watering.

3 Choose herbs that will not grow too large and that have a small rootball so that they are easy to fit through the holes. The plants here are chives, thymes, wild strawberry and a bigger plant of golden marjoram for the top.

4 Carefully feed the plant through the hole, making sure that you do not damage the roots. This can be done from the inside, teasing the foliage through, or from the outside, pushing the roots in.

5 Water thoroughly, taking care to avoid splashing compost (potting soil) out of the holes. Keep well watered. The pot may be placed on a terracotta dish and watered from the bottom as well as from the top.

Care and maintenance

■ RIGHT
Pruning sage regularly ensures fresh, new growth each year.

■ RIGHT
Pruning sage regularly ensures fresh, new growth each year.

Herbs that grow in the wild on stony, sunbaked hillsides will produce a stronger concentration of essential oils in their leaves if left unfertilized. These herbs revel in a mulch of gravel which sets them off attractively and keeps their leaves and necks dry in winter, while reducing the need for weeding. Those herbs from cooler areas, for example sweet cicely and comfrey, like to have a mulch of well-rotted manure or compost in winter when their stems have died down.

Shrubby herbs, such as lavender, thyme and sage, benefit from pruning. They produce fresh, new growth each year, the previous year's growth having become brown and woody. Simply cut all the branches to just above the woody part to keep the bush compact. If this is carried out every spring from the second year onward, the result will be a healthy, well-maintained plant. All too often gardeners leave sage unattended for several years and then want to prune back a straggly plant, but doing this can be fatal.

A word of warning about rue is needed. This pretty, delicately leaved plant looks very attractive but must be pruned in early spring only on an overcast day. The sap reacts with sunlight to produce unpleasant skin blisters, and the marks they leave take several months to disappear.

Culinary herbs may need cutting back once or twice during the growing season in order to prevent them from flowering; they will produce plenty of succulent, new shoots for cooking instead. Fennel, chives, sorrel, marjoram and lemon balm benefit from this action. When

PRUNING COTTON LAVENDER

1 This green-leaved variety of cotton lavender (*Santolina rosmarinifolia*) is in need of pruning to regain its shape.

2 Using a pair of shears, start clipping, making sure that there is plenty of greenery below the cut stems.

3 Step back from the bush occasionally to make sure that you are clipping it into a rounded shape from all angles.

CUTTING BACK FENNEL

1 Unchecked, fennel will grow to head-height, become coarse in stem and leaf and produce seed. If cut back early, it will make plenty of young growth for cooking.

2 Using sharp secateurs (shears), cut the stems down almost to ground level.

3 The leaves that have been cut can be put in the freezer for later use. Chives can also be cut back in this way.

---

a plant flowers, all its resources go into producing seeds and the leaves become coarser and tired-looking. By cutting back you can also prevent self-seeding, which in some varieties may become a nuisance.

Angelica is slightly unusual in that it is monocarpic. This means that it dies after flowering. By removing the flower buds and preventing this from happening you can prolong its life. However, if angelica is allowed to

seed, it produces magnificent seed-heads and huge supplies of seed for growing more plants.

When harvesting chives you can include the flowers: they make a colourful addition to salads.

4 The cotton lavender is now pruned into a dome shape and will quickly put on new growth. Clipping twice a year keeps the bush compact and shapely.

■ **LEFT** Angelica grows best in rich, damp soil, but tolerates most conditions, provided it is not too dry. Grow in a semi-shaded situation.

Harvesting

One of the greatest pleasures is picking herbs fresh from the garden, enjoying the scent of rosemary or sage as you take it to the kitchen for cooking. Herbs usually have the most flavour just before they come into flower, making this the ideal time for harvesting. As you pick from shrubs such as thyme and hyssop, cut from all over the bush to keep it compact and shapely, thus pruning at the same time as harvesting.

There are several methods for preserving the delicious flavour of herbs for the winter. The easiest is to dry them by picking sprigs in the morning, when any moisture from the night has evaporated but before the heat of the sun has started to release the oils from the leaves. They should be gathered in individual bunches and secured with an elastic (rubber) band.

■ ABOVE
These lovage leaves have been dried and are ready for storing in a dark glass jar.

HARVESTING MARJORAM

1 Marjoram is easily air dried. Cut bunches of healthy material at mid-morning on a dry day.

2 Strip off the lower leaves, which would otherwise become crushed and damaged once bunched.

Storing herbs

Hang them in a warm, dry place with good air circulation and out of sunlight, which would fade them and damage their flavour.

Once dry, the bunches can be easily stripped of their leaves which are stored in dark glass jars, and labelled with their name and the date. Although it looks attractive to see bunches of herbs hanging from the kitchen ceiling, neither this nor storage in clear glass jars will preserve their flavour. Dried herbs should be used within the year, and new bunches harvested next summer.

Not all herbs dry well, parsley, chervil and tarragon among them, so the modern method of freezing is ideal for some of the more delicate flavours. A quick way is to chop the leaves, mix them with water and freeze as ice cubes, which can then be added during cooking as required. The large leaves of basil can be picked off the stems and frozen in small plastic bags. For smaller-leaved herbs such as tarragon and chervil, whole sprigs can be frozen.

3 Twist an elastic (rubber) band around the stems to hold them tightly together.

4 Gather as many bunches as you need, then the bunches can be hung in a dry, airy place where they are protected from light.

■ BELOW
The scented heads of lavender and the pungent tops of marjoram are very easily air dried.

Oils and vinegars

Both oils and vinegars will absorb the flavour of an individual herb and this is a delightful way of preserving the tastes of summer. Herb oils and vinegars make attractive gifts. However, the making of herbal oils is best left to commercial manufacturers as there is a risk of botulism. This is not the case with vinegars, which can be safely made by steeping sprigs of rosemary or tarragon in wine vinegar. This is then sealed tightly with a cork in a glass bottle and left for 3 weeks.

■ BELOW
Herbal oils and vinegars look lovely and
make wonderful presents.

HERBS FOR OILS (O) AND VINEGARS (V)

Basil OV

Dill V

French tarragon V

Garlic OV

Horseradish V

Mint V

Rosemary O

Salad burnet V

Thyme O

CULINARY HERBS THAT DRY SUCCESSFULLY

Bay

Hyssop

Marjoram

Rosemary

Sage

Thyme

Winter savory

HERBS FOR FREEZING

Basil

Chervil

Chives

Dill

Fennel

French tarragon

Lemon balm

Mint

Parsley

Propagation

Division

Producing your own plants is immensely satisfying, and there are several different ways of doing this. The easiest is by division, which is used to multiply herbs that form clumps of rooted stems, and involves splitting the crown of an existing plant. This applies to the herbaceous herbs and is done when the plant has died down for the winter or in early spring as growth revives.

Using a fork, dig up the clump or part of the clump and break it up manually into suitable-sized pieces for replanting. If you do this in spring when the plant has started to grow again, cut the stems down to 2.5cm (1in) before planting and keep them watered thoroughly.

■ LEFT
Lift and divide chives every 3-5 years according to growth. Pot up in autumn for forcing winter supplies indoors.

DIVIDING A CLUMP OF CHIVES

1 Although traditionally herbaceous herbs are divided in winter, chives can be split during the growing season. Dig up a clump of healthy chives, having first prepared a new piece of ground.

2 Cut the tops down to a few centimetres to make them easier to handle and because the leaves would otherwise wilt.

3 It is now easy to pull the clump apart just using your hands.

4 From a good-sized clump all these smaller clumps have been produced, each with about ten stems.

5 Replant the new clumps of chives with a gap of 25cm (10in) between plants. Water well and they will quickly regrow.

Softwood cuttings

Spring, when herbs are growing vigorously, is the perfect time to take softwood cuttings from the new season's growth. This is particularly appropriate for the bushy herbs that cannot be propagated by division. Using secateurs (shears) or a knife, cut off growing tips by about 13–15cm (5–6in). Then trim below a leaf joint and strip off the bottom leaves until just the top leaves are left so that there is not too large a surface for moisture loss. The resultant cutting should be approximately 10cm (4in) long.

Put a group of cuttings into a mixture of 50 per cent sand and 50 per cent coir or peat in a pot or divided plug tray, and cover with polythene (plastic) to keep them moist. When roots begin to appear from the bottom of the pot, they are ready to be potted on, using this time a potting compost (potting soil) which contains the appropriate nutrients. Taking softwood cuttings is the only reliable method for propagating cultivars such as variegated forms of thymes and marjorams to ensure that they remain true to the original plant.

Seed sowing

Raising plants from seed is rewarding and cheap, whether for the perennials or annuals that are in demand for cooking. Sow seed thinly in seed compost, using plug trays to avoid the fiddly business of thinning out and to minimize root disturbance when potting on. This suits borage, dill and chervil in particular. Alternatively, sow directly into the ground in a well-prepared seed bed in spring. Parsley must be sown only when the soil has warmed up, and trying too early can result in poor germination.

TAKING SOFTWOOD CUTTINGS

1 Purple sage can be propagated by softwood cuttings in spring. Using secateurs (shears) or a knife, take 13–15cm/5–6in long cuttings of the growing tips.

SEED SOWING IN A DIVIDED PLUG TRAY

1 For herbs such as borage that resent root disturbance, sowing seed into a plug tray is ideal. Fill the tray with a proprietary seed compost.

2 Borage seeds are large and can be individually handled. Put two seeds into each module (section) of the plug tray.

2 Trim each cutting just below a leaf joint. The secateurs (shears) must be sharp to get a good, clean cut.

3 Strip off the lower leaves, taking care not to damage the main stem.

4 Insert the cuttings into compost either in pots or, as here, in divided polystyrene plug (divided) trays. Water with a fine mist and cover with a plastic propagator lid so that they do not dry out.

3 Lightly cover with a thin layer of compost and label with the name and the date of sowing.

4 Set the plug tray on capillary matting and keep watered from below. The result is healthy, young borage plants.

5 The advantage of seed sowing in a plug tray can be seen from this borage seedling. It has good root development in its individual section of compost, which will not be disturbed on planting.

Calendar

Early spring

Buy seeds for the coming year. Start sowing hardy herbs under glass. Divide herbaceous perennials as the shoots start to reappear, replanting in weed-free soil.

Mid-spring

Take softwood cuttings of bushy herbs like lavender and thyme, and of perennials such as lemon balm and mint. Replace worn-out bushes of lavender, sage and thyme. Order divided plug trays of young plants.

Late spring

Sow annual herb seeds directly into the soil once it is warm enough. Make successive sowings of parsley, dill and chervil so there are plenty for harvesting during the season. Put tender herbs, such as bay trees, out-side for the summer once the frosts have finished. Keep all containers well watered. Prepare tubs and hanging baskets with selections of herbs.

Early summer

Be vigilant over greenhouse pests and, if necessary, order biological controls. Pinch off the growing tips of basil to make bushy plants. Clip box hedges, using lengths of string as a guide. Also clip topiary to maintain shape. Prune cotton lavender to create silvery mounds.

Mid- to late summer

Water newly planted herbs every day. Pick bunches of lavender and other scented herbs for drying. Clip lavender shrubs to maintain neat bushes. Harvest and dry flowers for winter arrangements. Preserve summer flavours by freezing or drying herbs or by steeping them in vinegars or oils.

Culinary herbs can be harvested throughout the summer for immediate use or for drying and storing.

heavy soil to improve drainage over the winter. Mulch bushy herbs with gravel to keep their necks dry.

Winter

Clear away dead leaves, especially from around bushy herbs. Dig over the garden so the frost can break up the soil. Clean the greenhouse, washing down the glass and removing plant debris that might harbour pests. Put your feet up, have a cup of tea and go through the seed catalogues, planning next year's crop.

Early autumn

Start saving seed as the plants mature, storing it in labelled paper bags in a dry place. Leave some seedheads for the birds and for the structure they give the winter garden. Bring tender herbs into the greenhouse for protection before frosts start.

Mid- to late autumn

Cut herbaceous herbs down to a crown once their stems have died back. Alternatively, leave dead stems to protect crowns from frost and provide sanctuary for overwintering ladybirds. Mix gravel into areas of

■ LEFT
These drying herbs have paper covers to protect them from light and dust.

Pests and diseases

Fortunately, herbs grown outside are generally free from pests and diseases. Buying strong, healthy plants in the first place, thinning out seedlings so that they are not overcrowded, and keeping plants well weeded are all ways of keeping pests and diseases at bay. There are, however, a few possible problems to look out for.

Greenhouse pests and diseases

How to identify: Herbs grown in the greenhouse may suffer from a variety of pests and diseases, which occur whenever plants are cultivated in closed conditions. Check plants regularly for infestation by pests; the presence of fine webs and damaged leaves may be the first sign.

Control and prevention: If herbs are destined for cooking, it would be unwise to use chemical sprays, but there are biological controls available. These take the form of predatory insects, which can be released into the greenhouse where they will attack the offending pest. It is now easy to order through the mail biological controls for red spider mite, whitefly, aphids, thrips and vine weevil, caterpillars and the scale insects that may attack bay trees.

Good hygiene in the greenhouse is important to help prevent pests and diseases from gaining a foothold, and this involves clearing away any dead leaves, a thorough cleaning over the winter and making sure that plants are adequately watered to keep them healthy. Ventilation and careful observation of your plants is essential.

Mint rust

How to identify: Mint, especially when grown in full sun, can develop a fungal infection known as mint rust. The leaves become covered in orange blotches which eventually cause them to drop off. Fungal spores will then lie on the soil surface over winter.

Control and prevention: Cut off and burn every emerging shoot for an entire growing season and cover the soil with straw in winter and then burn it. This kills the spores but does not damage the plant's roots. To avoid rust attack in the first place, grow mint out of direct sunlight.

Scorching

How to identify: Golden-leaved plants grown in full sun may suffer scorching on their leaves.

Control and prevention: Take care to grow certain herbs in semi-shade, in particular, golden marjoram, golden lemon balm and ginger mint. Golden sage and golden thyme have thicker leaves and can stand more light.

Other recommended herbs

Aloe vera
A tender plant, native to Africa, this has thick, fleshy leaves and a clump-forming habit, making it an unusual houseplant. Short, white lines

Aloe vera

mark the spiky foliage and it has tubular, yellow flowers in summer. The sap from its broken leaves will soothe burns, especially sunburn. Propagate by offsets. Height 60cm (2ft). Perennial.

Anise hyssop
Agastache foeniculum This handsome plant is most useful in the garden as its aromatic leaves and bold spikes of purple flowers in summer attract hover flies to the garden which in turn eat aphids. The aniseed-scented leaves can be dried for pot-pourri or eaten in salads.

They can also be made into a refreshing herb tea. Height 90cm (3ft). Perennial.

Curry plant
Helichrysum italicum A native of southern Europe, this silvery herb has curry-smelling leaves whose scent hangs in an enclosed garden on a sunny day, especially just after rain. Normally grown as a decorative plant for its attractive foliage and yellow flowers in summer, its leaves can also be used to flavour salads and rice dishes. Grow in light, well-drained soil. The flowers dry well and are useful for winter decoration and also has insect-repellent properties. Height 60cm (2ft). Shrub.

Curry plant

Garlic:
Allium sativum An essential flavouring in Mediterranean and Eastern cooking, garlic

gives a pungency and strength to tomato dishes, soups, curries, mayonnaise, sauces and oils. Individual cloves are broken from garlic bulbs for planting. They like well-drained soil and a sunny position, and will flower in late summer. Garlic has long been used for medicinal purposes because of its antibacterial and antiseptic properties, the best results being from the fresh bulb. Height 60cm (2ft). Bulb.

Garlic chives
Allium tuberosum Garlic chives make a tasty alternative to common chives, having flat leaves with a mild garlic flavour. They are particularly good in salads, with cream cheeses and in omelettes. The white, starry flowers appear in late summer and can be broken into individual florets for decorating salads. Height 50cm (20in). Bulb.

Wild garlic
Allium ursinum A superb sight in northern woods in spring, the wide, fresh green leaves and white, starry flowers of wild garlic can completely carpet the ground under trees. A walk through such woods is memorable for the strong scent of garlic. The leaves can be used in soups and stews, in vegetable curries and omelettes. Height 40cm (16in). Perennial.

Lavender:
Lavandula angustifolia Known as English lavender but a native of the Mediterranean, this is a classic cottage-garden plant. The essential oil

Lemon grass

is strongly antiseptic and known to kill bacteria. Height 90cm (3ft). Shrub.
Lavandula angustifolia 'Hidcote Pink' A dwarf lavender with grey foliage and pink flowers, valued for its soft effect. Height 60cm (2ft). Shrub.

Lemon grass
Cymbopogon citratus The leaves of this aromatic grass give a delicious taste of lemon to Asian cooking and are used in stir-fries, with vegetables, fish and chicken, and to make a tangy herb tea. Now available in packs of cut leaf

bases in supermarkets, it is rapidly gaining in popularity. Being tender, it needs greenhouse conditions in many areas. Height 1.5m (5ft). Perennial.

Lemon verbena

Lemon verbena
Aloysia triphylla For an even more intense lemon scent, lemon verbena is a must. Though requiring greenhouse protection in some areas, it is easily grown, making a deciduous shrub, whose branches are pruned back to the main stem in late autumn. Tiny, white flowers bloom in summer and the leaves are gathered to make a tangy, refreshing herb tea. The dried leaves can retain their lemon scent for several years and are ideal for pot-pourri. Height up to 3m (10ft). Shrub.

Marigold
Calendula officinalis With its brilliant orange flowers, the marigold is synonymous with summer gardens. Its flowers can be used in dyeing cloth or in cooking rice for a saffron colour. A hardy plant, it has strongly scented leaves and will self-seed. A valuable skin healer, calendula cream is soothing for sunburn and used in homeopathy. Height 70cm (28in). Annual.

Marjoram
Origanum majorana This herb is known as sweet marjoram because of its sweet yet spicy flavour, or knotted marjoram, because of the appearance of its tight flower buds. Forming an important part of Italian and Greek cooking, it enhances

Rue

soups, pasta and meats. Height 30cm (1ft). Perennial grown as an annual in cold areas.

Marshmallow
Althaea officinalis The marshmallows sold as sweets (candy) are made with egg white, flour and sugar, but this pretty plant was originally

Tricolor sage

the basis for marshmallow balls sucked as sweets (candy) or soothing throat lozenges. The long roots are high in mucilage and, when boiled, release half their weight in a thick gum that was made into a soft confectionery paste. Tall stems carry velvety, soft leaves and pink flowers in late summer. Height 90cm (3ft). Perennial.

Mint: Corsican Mint
Mentha requienii One of the tiniest herbs, yet one of the most strongly scented, the little, creeping Corsican mint has the most minute, lilac flowers in summer. Its size makes it suitable for a herb pot or windowbox, rock garden or filler between paving stones. Height 2cm (¾in). Perennial.

Water mint
Mentha aquatica Ponds provide small oases for wildlife and the very fragrant-leaved water mint can be planted in the margins or in boggy areas. The leaves are dark with a purple tinge and purple veins; the mauve flowers are borne in summer. Height 90cm (3ft). Perennial.

Mullein
Verbascum thapsus Mullein, with its tall, yellow spires of flowers, provides height in the herb garden and self-seeds abundantly, though it is easy to pull up where it is not wanted. The first year sees a basal rosette of wonderfully woolly and silvery leaves; in the second year, being a biennial, it sends up its dramatic flower spike. It is also known as the candlewick plant, since its stems were once used as wicks in candle making. The leaves can be smoked to ease coughs or as a tobacco substitute. Height 2m (6ft). Biennial.

Myrtle
Myrtus communis Queen Victoria had sprigs of myrtle in her wedding bouquet, this herb being an ancient symbol of love, dedicated by the

Romans to the goddess Venus. Being somewhat tender, this sweetly scented shrub needs a sunny, sheltered position or greenhouse cultivation. White, starry

Clary sage

flowers in early summer are followed by blue-black berries which, when dried, can flavour meats. Height up to 3m (10ft). Shrub.

Peppermint
Mentha x *piperita* The best of all the mints for making mint tea, peppermint has strong-tasting leaves that act on the digestive system, making it valuable for a wide range of conditions. Commercially it is of importance as a flavouring in sweets and chocolates, in toothpastes, indigestion remedies and liqueurs. Like other mints, it is a rapid

spreader and can be invasive. The toothed leaves are somewhat purplish, and the flowers are pale mauve. Height 90cm (3ft). Perennial.

Purple coneflower
Echinacea angustifolia A beautiful border plant, the purple coneflower has deep pinkish-purple petals radiating from a brown raised centre. Used for centuries by the native North Americans, it has recently been the subject of much interest for its ability to boost the immune system. It is the roots that are harvested for medicinal purposes, and purple coneflower can now be bought in pill form from

Woolly thyme

health shops for treating conditions such as sore throats and colds. Height 1.2m (4ft). Perennial.

Rue
Ruta graveolens Bitter-smelling rue has pretty, blue-green leaves and small, yellow flowers in summer. It makes an attractive border plant, combining well with stronger colours. Historically, it was laid on the floors of jails to keep fleas away and it was also used to ward off witches. Rue should always be handled with care as the sap reacts with sunlight to produce unpleasant skin blisters. Height 45cm (1 1/2ft). Shrub.

Sage: Clary sage
Salvia sclarea var. *turkestanica* Quite different in appearance from the shrubby sages, clary sports pale blue flowers in larger pink bracts on tall stems. It makes a lovely fuzz of pinky purple in a garden border, and the whole plant is strongly aromatic. Grow in sandy, reasonably moist soil. Height 90cm (3ft). Biennial.

Pineapple sage
Salvia elegans 'Scarlet Pineapple'. The leaves of this form of sage have a lovely scent of pineapple, hence its name. The brilliant red flowers appear in winter. It is not hardy, but makes a very attractive houseplant if grown in a large tub. The leaves can be used in puddings or added to fruit drinks. Height 90cm (3ft). Perennial.

Tricolor sage
Salvia officinalis 'Tricolor' This sage has three-coloured leaves of green variegated with white and pink. It is lower-growing than common sage

Wall germander

and is a good plant for a pot. Height 45cm (1 1/2ft). Shrub.

Salad burnet
Sanguisorba minor Native to Europe and Asia, salad burnet is a traditional herb-garden plant. It has pretty little pairs of leaves and wine-red, globular flowers on thin stems. One of the earliest herbs to be harvested in spring, its leaves have a nutty, cucumber-like taste suitable for salads and garnishes. Traditionally steeped in wine cups, it can be used like borage in fruit drinks. Height 40cm (16in). Perennial.

Tansy

Tanacetum vulgare With ferny foliage and bright yellow, button flowers, tansy is an attractive if rampant plant for the herb or cottage

Tansy

garden. It has a strong-smelling leaf which acts as an insecticide, and was strewn on medieval floors for this reason. Its peppery taste adds heat to cakes, puddings and omelettes, but large amounts are toxic. Never take during pregnancy. Height 90cm (3ft). Perennial.

Thyme: Wild Thyme

Thymus serpyllum This plant has given rise to numerous excellent cultivars. The species has purple flowers in summer, but its cultivars can range from white, pink, deep pink, through to crimson or even

salmon-pink. It carpets the ground and is perfect for growing in the cracks of terraced areas. Height 2cm (¾in). Prostrate shrub.

Woolly thyme

Thymus pseudolanuginosus The woolly thyme is a strong growing carpeting herb with grey coloured hairy leaves giving the appearance of closely cropped sheep's wool.

Valerian

Valeriana officinalis Valerian grows wild in wet, swampy places, its pale, pink clusters of flowers waving on tall stems above divided leaves. As a sedative, tincture of valerian was given to soldiers suffering

Woad

from shell shock after World War I (the rhizomes have a medicinal value). Height 1.5m (5ft). Perennial.

Wall germander

Teucrium chamaedrys A pretty, compact shrub, wall germander has glossy, dark green leaves and pink flowers in late summer. It makes a nice low herb hedge in a knot garden, and its leaves are an ingredient of vermouth. Use externally as a mouthwash for gum disease, but do not take internally. Height 25cm (10in). Perennial.

Winter savory

Satureja montana Like summer savory, this evergreen, shrubby herb is cooked with all kinds of beans, its flavour being sharper and more like that of thyme. It has pale, bluish flowers late in the summer, and can be clipped into a neat mound or planted as a dwarf hedge. It thrives in a sunny position in well-drained soil. Height 40cm (16in). Shrub.

Woad

Isatis tinctoria The famous dye plant, woad gives no indication of the blue colour that can be extracted from its grey-green leaves and yellow flowering tops that bloom in early summer. Ancient Britons painted it on their bodies to scare their enemies in battle. It was used as a dye for centuries until superseded by the use of indigo. Height 1.2m (4ft). Biennial or short-lived perennial.

Yarrow

Achillea millefolium Named after Achilles, who reputedly staunched his soldiers' wounds with its leaves, yarrow has a long tradition as a

Yarrow

healing herb. The finely divided leaves look ferny, and stout stems bear flat-topped, white or pink flowers in summer. An infusion of the leaves reduces temperature. Height 60cm (2ft). Perennial.

Yellow flag

Iris pseudacorus The bright yellow flowers of the yellow flag iris bloom in summer and provide colour for the edges of ponds and boggy areas. It combines especially well in the garden with blue flowers. The roots yield a black dye and the flowers a yellow dye. Height 1.2m (4ft). Perennial.

Index

■ LEFT
Wild garlic

ACKNOWLEDGEMENTS
The publishers would like to
thank the following nurseries
for their help in the
production of this book:
Hollington and Hexham
Herbs. All photographs were
taken by Andrea Jones with
the exception of the
following: Peter Anderson
page 15(tr), E.T. Archive page
10(bl), John Freeman page
11, Michelle Garrett pages 4,
9(b), 10(tr), 16(b), 45, 50(bl),
and 57(both), and Polly
Wreford pages 19(t), 51(br),
and 52.

■ LEFT
**Bay is an ideal tree for a mixed
border or for softening the
impact of a brick wall.**